OUR VOLCANIC PLANET

Written by Jilly Hunt
Illustrated by Evelline Andrya

Contents

OXFORD
UNIVERSITY PRESS

Words to look out for ...

familiarize *VERB*

To familiarize yourself with something is to make sure you know about it.

habit *NOUN*

something that you do often

minimum *NOUN*

the smallest number or amount possible

precise *ADJECTIVE*

exact

sensible *ADJECTIVE*

A sensible person or thing is wise or shows common sense.

suggest *VERB*

If something suggests that something will happen, it makes you think that it will happen.

What are volcanoes?

How much do you know about volcanoes?

You probably know they are very hot. You might know they can be very noisy. They are also smelly. They can even explode!

A volcano is an opening in the Earth's crust. The crust is the thick surface of the Earth. Underneath the crust, there is hot liquid rock. This is called magma.

Magma, **gas** and **ash** can escape through an opening in the crust. This is called an eruption.

Eruptions can be powerful enough to burst high into the sky.

Parts of a volcano

crater: the main opening

lava: hot liquid rock after it reaches the surface

magma chamber: a large pool of hot liquid rock under a volcano

main vent: the tube that connects the magma to the surface

Types of volcano

Volcanoes can be active, dormant or extinct.

- Active volcanoes are likely to erupt again.

- Dormant volcanoes have not erupted for a long time. They are unlikely to erupt soon, but may do in the future.

- Extinct volcanoes erupted a very long time ago. Nothing suggests they'll erupt again.

There are more than 1000 active volcanoes in the world!

If something suggests that something will happen, it makes you think that it will happen.

Mauna Loa

Pacific Ocean

🌋 volcanoes in the 'Ring of Fire'

Most active volcanoes are found around the warm Pacific Ocean. This is called the 'Ring of Fire'.

One of Earth's tallest active volcanoes is Mauna Loa. More than half of Mauna Loa is under the sea. Its **base** sits on the ocean floor.

Life by a volcano

Living near a volcano can be dangerous. A volcanic eruption can cause a lot of damage.

Lava can **destroy** buildings, roads, crops and forests. **Poisonous** gases can harm people, plants and animals.

Sometimes lava flows slowly. Scientists can watch these eruptions from a safe distance.

Sometimes, volcanic eruptions can cause huge waves of water called tsunamis.

Tsunamis can travel a long way and can travel quickly. These powerful waves can move as fast as a jet plane.

It might not seem <u>sensible</u> to live near an active volcano. However, lots of people do live near volcanoes.

There are many **benefits**:

- The dark soil on the slopes around a volcano is good for growing food.

- Visitors pay **local** people money to take them to see the volcano.

- Visitors spend money in local shops.

This man is **ploughing** a rice field near a volcano.

A <u>sensible</u> person or thing is wise or shows common sense.

Some animals also live near volcanoes.

This lake is in Tanzania, Africa. Flamingos have a habit of coming back to the lake each year.

The volcano makes the water in the lake **toxic**. It would burn our skin, but flamingos have tougher skin. They are safe as not many **predators** can survive here.

This iguana lays its eggs near a volcano. The hot ash from the volcano helps to keep the iguana's eggs warm.

A habit is something that you do often.

Volcanic legends

Today, science helps us to understand volcanic eruptions. In the past, people had other ways of explaining them.

The island of Hawaii is in the Pacific Ocean. There are four active volcanoes on it. People there tell stories of Pele, the Hawaiian **goddess** of fire and volcanoes. They believe Pele created the volcanic Hawaiian islands.

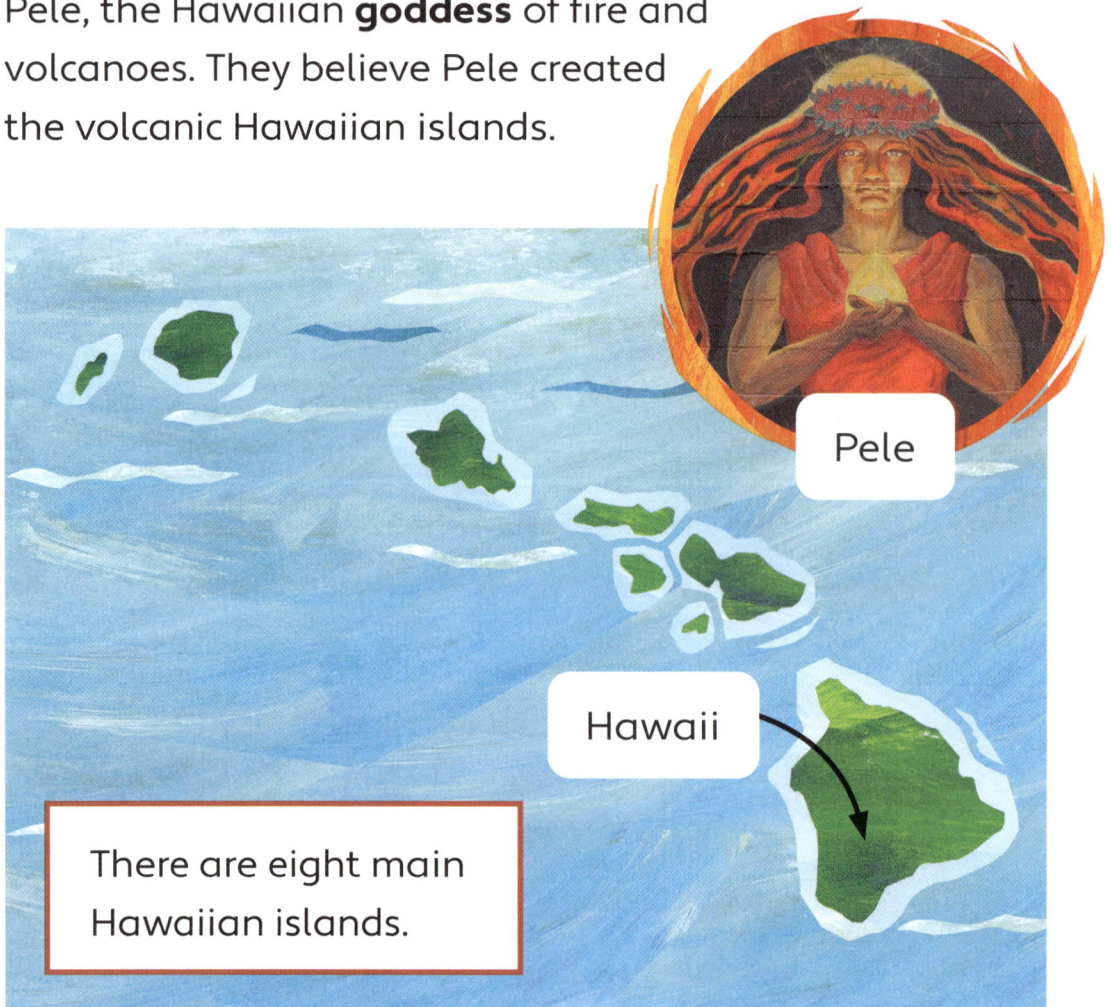

Pele

Hawaii

There are eight main Hawaiian islands.

Around 2500 years ago, the ancient **Romans** believed in many gods. They left gifts for Vulcan, their god of fire. They hoped he would protect them from volcanic eruptions.

The Romans came from the city of Rome in Italy.

Italy

Rome

The word 'volcano' comes from 'Vulcan'. Ancient Romans believed Vulcan lived in a volcano. They thought if Vulcan became angry, the volcano would erupt.

Vulcan

Eruptions from long ago

We don't have precise records of past eruptions. However, we do have art that shows what people saw.

This painting in a cave in France may show an ancient volcanic eruption.

This drawing shows the eruption of Mount Asama in Japan in 1783.

Smoke from Mount Asama is shown in this picture from 1859.

Something is precise when it is exact.

Some written documents tell us about living through an eruption.

Around 2000 years ago in Italy, Mount Vesuvius erupted. It destroyed the city of Pompeii (say: pom-pay).

A writer called Pliny the Younger wrote about it at the time.

These are some of the ruins of Pompeii in front of Mount Vesuvius.

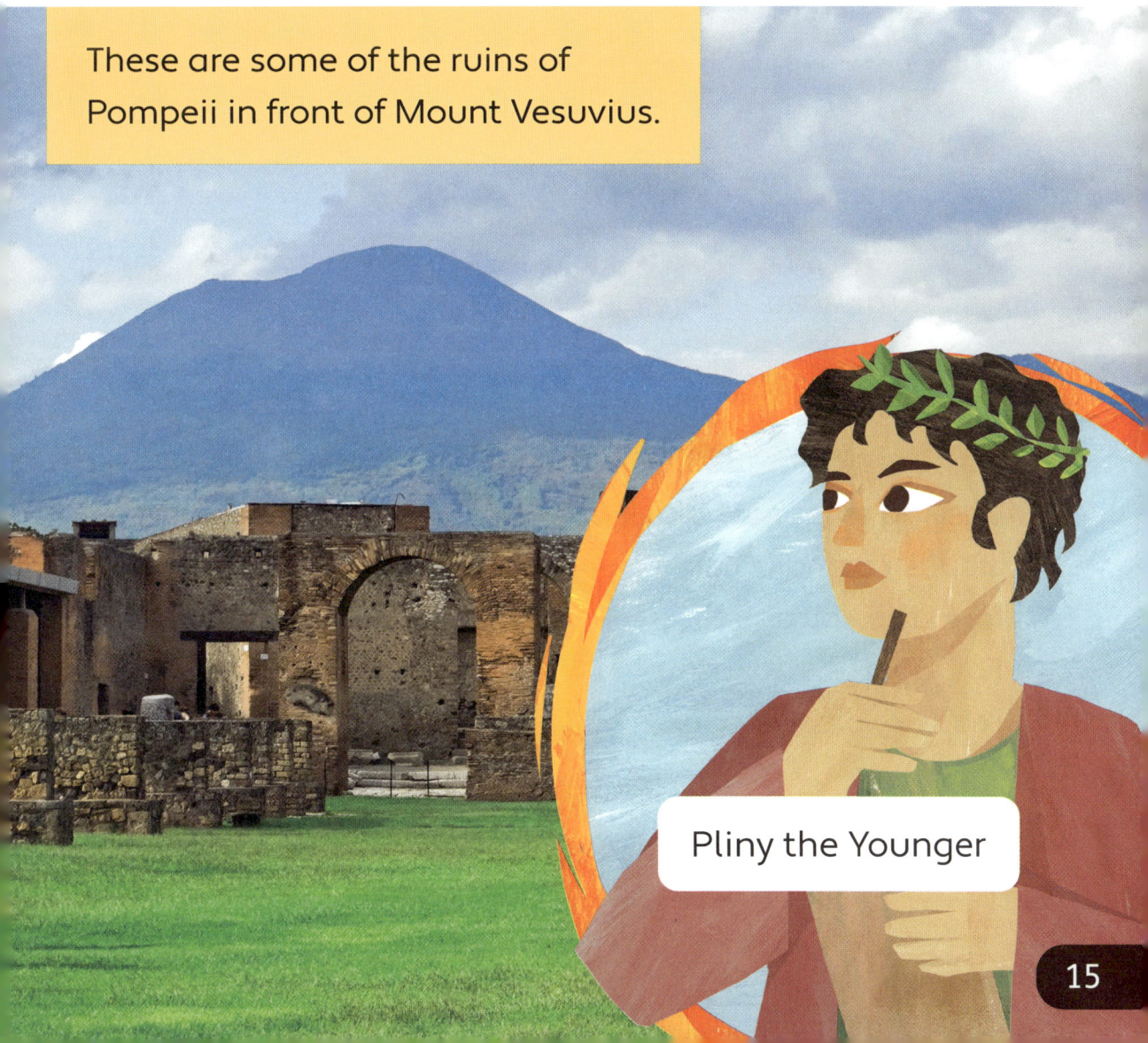

Pliny the Younger

Krakatau: A mighty eruption

Krakatau (say: krak-uh-tou) is a volcano in Indonesia.

Krakatau

In the spring of 1883, passing ships saw black clouds of smoke coming from the volcano.
For months, Krakatau made explosive noises.

Krakatau is sometimes called Krakatoa.

Then one morning, there was a sound louder than anything anyone had ever heard. The noise was even heard in faraway countries. It was the final explosion of Krakatau as it collapsed into the sea.

Krakatau's collapse created huge tsunamis. Thousands of people died and many towns and villages were destroyed.

This ship was washed onto land by a tsunami.

This is a report from someone who saw a tsunami.

I saw in the distance an enormous, black-looking mass of water. It appeared mountains high, and it rushed on with a fearful roar. At the next moment, I was swept off my feet. I found myself struggling in the water.

Krakatau: Around the world

The eruption of Krakatau was seen around the world.

Ash clouds blocked the sun's light over a huge area. The darkness lasted for a minimum of two and a half days.

It was reported that animals were confused about whether it was day or night.

A minimum of something is the smallest number or amount possible.

For many months after the eruption, the colour of the sky in the evening was different. Volcanic dust changed the light.

The changes made by the volcanic dust created amazing sunsets.

These paintings show what the sunsets looked like.

Child of Krakatau

The explosion of Krakatau in 1883 destroyed most of the volcano. Around 30 years later, a new cone appeared. People called it Anak Krakatau, meaning 'child of Krakatau'.

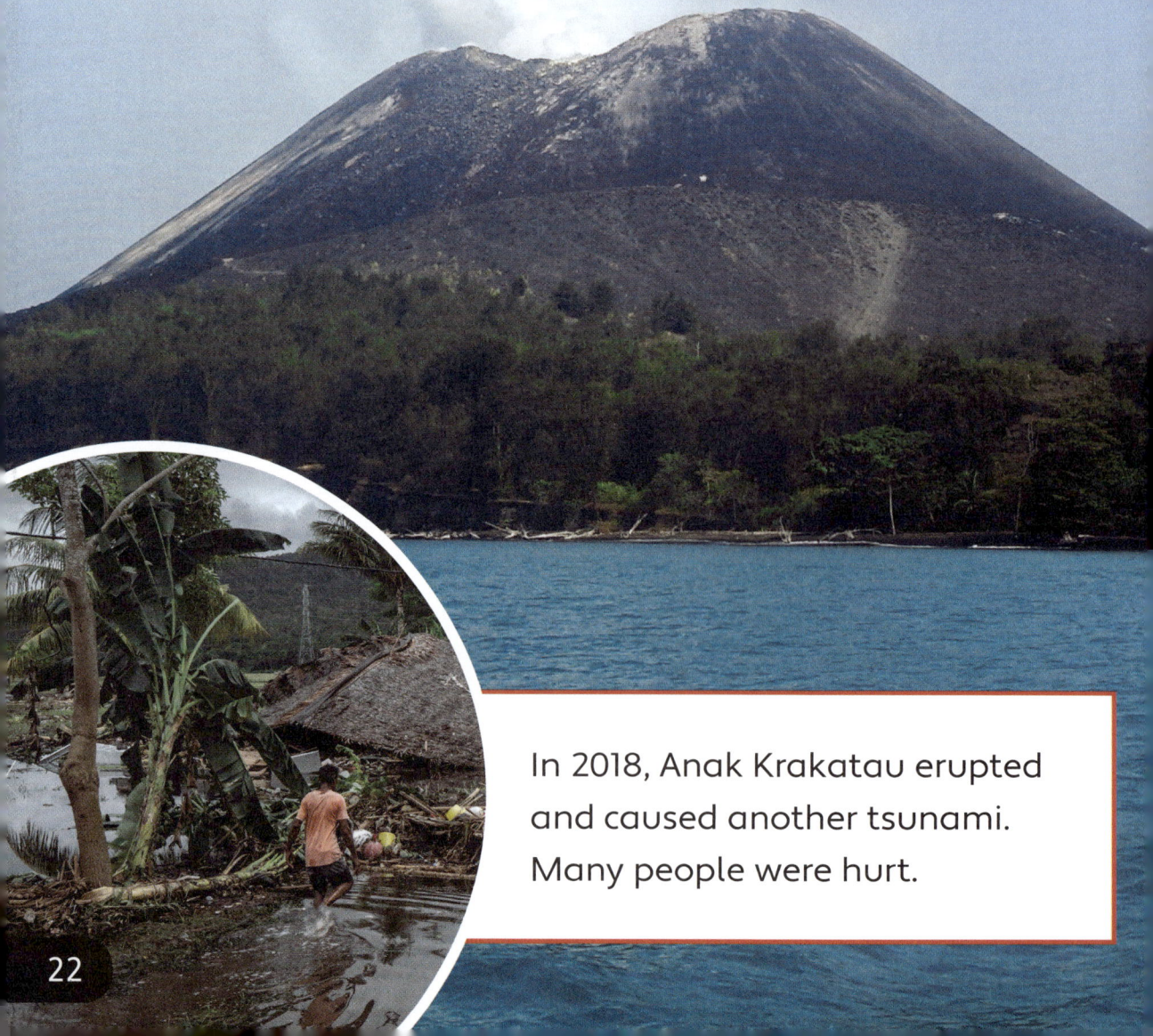

In 2018, Anak Krakatau erupted and caused another tsunami. Many people were hurt.

Staying safe near volcanoes

Around the world, there are different volcano warnings in place.

People living near volcanoes <u>familiarize</u> themselves with these different warnings.

This road sign tells people that there is a volcano in the area.

This warning system makes a loud noise. It tells people to leave an area due to an eruption.

These warnings can save many lives.

To <u>familiarize</u> yourself with something is to make sure you know about it.

Glossary

ash: the powder that is left after something has been burned

base: the bottom of a mountain

benefits: something that is useful or helpful

destroy: to destroy something is to ruin it

gas: something that is not liquid or solid, such as oxygen

goddess: a female god

local: someone who lives in a particular place

ploughing: turning soil over with a plough, which is a tool used in farming

poisonous: able to cause illness or death if swallowed or breathed in

predators: animals that hunt and eat other animals

Romans: a large and powerful group of people who ruled countries around the world thousands of years ago

toxic: damaging to the body, including being poisonous

Index